Restarting Your Business After the Pandemic

By

Robert Villegas

Restarting Your Business After the Pandemic

By Robert Villegas

© Copyright 2020 by Robert Villegas

All rights reserved. No part of this book may be reproduced in any form without the prior written consent of the copyright holder and/or his representative/s.

ISBN: 9798645553838

Imprint: Independently published

Published in the United States of America by

Document Services International

Series Title: Villegas Business Volume 4

www.documentservicesinternational.com

www.robertvillegas.com

Contact: robertsswot@outlook.com

Table of Contents

Restarting Your Business 4
The SWOT Analysis 6
SMART Goals 6
Before You Begin: A Checklist 9
    SWOT Analysis 26
Business Process Analysis 54
Villegas Decision-Making Worksheet 57
Villegas Problem Solving Worksheet 61
SWOT Analysis as a Performance Review 66
The Personal SWOT Analysis 68
Appendix: Checklists and Forms 69
    Restart Checklist Blank Form 69
    SMART Goals Worksheet 82
    Project Worksheet 86
    Villegas Decision-Making Worksheet 88
    Villegas Problem Solving Worksheet 91
    Performance Review 94
    Personal SWOT Analysis 95
    Remote Workers for your Business 97
Conclusion 101

Restarting Your Business

Your company has a problem. After weeks of being closed due to a government edict, you must decide whether you will open your company or close it completely. During the time off, you were given an "opportunity" to take out a grant from the Small Business Administration that you don't have to pay back if you had managed to use the money to pay the employees you had to lay off.

But you also needed money to pay rent and utilities and you don't know where you will get the income unless you open your business as soon as possible. What will you do?

As you look over your options, you learn that before you can open your business again, you must "ensure" that you follow a protocol prescribed by government that could mean you won't be earning money for some time – but you'll have to pay out a lot in the meantime.

If you are not able to perform your mandate to your customers because you cannot ensure you will make a profit you're going to have to get creative. This means the business processes that allowed your company to profit in the past no longer work. In short, if you don't successfully change your business mandate and business processes, the government will not allow you to go back into business.

You have also heard that a bevy of lawyers, not to mention the government, will be watching your every move. If you do the logical thing that will bring your business back, at any point in time, they may decree that you are violating the regulations they have put into place. Not only will government bureaucrats keep you from working but those lawyers may sue you for millions of dollars that you don't have if they can "prove" you are violating one of many new regulations designed to protect your employees from your new business model. In fact, you may be considered "selfish" for wanting to survive.

This problem has arisen during the course of the worldwide pandemic resulting from the release by a Chinese laboratory of the virus with one or more of their employees. It is something you may not have envisioned when you started the company; but it has come up and must be dealt with if your company is to continue.

Now, you, the business owner, are confronted with a major issue. What do you do about this problem? How are you going to make the problem go away? Is it even possible that the business can survive? It might be better if you closed down the business, divested yourself of your capital assets and started over with an entirely new business.

A SWOT Analysis is an objective look at the internal and external elements of your organization that impact your success or lack thereof. You need to perform this analysis if your business is going to survive because it will help you identify the changes you need to make in order to bring your business back. If done diligently, you will get a handle on what you need to do to save your business.

By analyzing and understanding the internal resources in your business going forward, you will gain a better understanding of what you need to do to take advantage of any new **S**trengths you can identify as well as how to overcome newly created **W**eaknesses. You will also understand how to plan for new **O**pportunities and especially the new **T**hreats that will impact your business in this completely new business environment. This analysis will give you crucial information for assessing the new external situations that now impact your business, local communities and the field in which you work.

The SWOT Analysis

This book is based upon my book "The SWOT Analysis Supercharged". However, I have included that book within this book so you won't have to buy it to understand the crucial concepts we will discuss.

Today, the SWOT Analysis is a logical approach to business management that can be applied to virtually any situation in any business entity. The SWOT Analysis is a staple of the business world that has been perfected countless times according to its own principles applied to itself. We will attempt to apply the SWOT Analysis to the specific issues you must address as you move forward to "re-imagine" your business model in the post-pandemic era.

SMART Goals

One of the innovations I have made to the SWOT Analysis is the insertion of SMART Goals to help you monitor and measure the actions you have decided to take. With this approach, you will first, do a "Restart Checklist" to get a grasp of the challenges brought forward by the pandemic and new government regulations, secondly, you will add suggest actions to your SWOT Analysis for evaluation and, thirdly, you will develop your SMART Goals, assign them to employees and then have them report back to you on the results of their activities.

As you engage your SWOT Analysis, you will integrate your solution activities using SMART rules and this will help you improve the prospects of success even more.

SMART stands for **S**pecific, **M**easurable, **A**chievable, **R**esults-Focused and **T**ime-bound goals. For instance, if you take a goal that you've developed out of a Weakness and make it Specific, Measurable, Achievable, Results-Focused and Time-bound, you can make some significant changes that will actually work for you.

Regarding this goal, here is an example of a goal you might establish for your business:

Specific: Sell more can openers.

Measurable: Sell 10 more can openers

Achievable: Yes, by explaining features better (Weakness: Sales presentation does not explain features fully)

Results-Focused: Yes

Time-bound: next week and thereafter. Report to your supervisor who will report to his boss.

As you can see, the integration of SWOT and SMART goals can improve sales which increases production and profits for the company. The manager can then advance to the step of informing his supervisors to ensure that every employee is able to fully explain all product features to customers. This will increase the overall effectiveness of the sales department. The data gathered from the SWOT Analysis in all categories can create a number of SMART goals which can be implemented company-wide thereby creating more sales and increasing job security and employee confidence.

I have written this book, as I did the previous book, to take an "old school" concept like the "SWOT Analysis" and supercharge it with the concept of SMART goals and project management principles. Through this approach, you will gain new insights, not only into your markets, but also other markets as well as new directions your company can take. By developing SMART goals to address the issues you uncover, you can re-start your company and innovate in a way not previously thought possible. Your results will be measurable and reportable to upper management as successes and improvements. Your company will change in measurable ways that are reflected in improved business processes or more sales.

As you will see, I have also included several forms which you can use with your team to record and share the activities you decide upon and keep track of how well the company is doing. These include the "Restart Checklist", the Business Process Analysis, Decision-Making Worksheet, Employee Performance Review and Personal SWOT Analysis. Finally, I have provided an example network system description should your company decide to allow employees to work remotely (from home or remote offices).

If you have new ideas or suggestions to add to this concept, by all means, let me know by emailing me at robertsswot@outlook.com. I guarantee that if your idea is added to future volumes of the book, you will receive complete credit.

Onward.

Before You Begin: A Checklist

This new Restart SWOT Analysis involves two specific analyses that you must undertake right now. The first involves identifying the specific challenges that the shutdown created for your business. To help with this we have provided a checklist of issues you should address before you re-open.

Once you finish this initial checklist, look over it carefully and make any change and adjustments you'd like before you present it to your management team or staff. This will serve as the basis for your SWOT Analysis.

First, you must identify as much as possible what the shutdown did to your business, not only to your customer base, but also your business and the market in which you operate, and what it will likely do in the future. Determine the business category for this question and place it under one of the SWOT Analyses, Strengths, Weaknesses, Opportunities and/or Threats.

_____
_____
_____
_____
_____
_____
_____

Are you going to have the same level of customer "churn" as you did in the past? What will be the "churn" rate for new customers be in the future and how can you manage this rate to ensure profitability? Determine the business category for this question and place it under one of the SWOT Analyses, Strengths, Weaknesses, Opportunities and/or Threats.

_____
_____
_____
_____
_____

_____
_____
_____

Next, what must you do in order to correct the loss of business and restore profitability? Determine the business category for this question and place it under one of the SWOT Analyses, Strengths, Weaknesses, Opportunities and/or Threats.

_____
_____
_____
_____
_____
_____
_____

So, let's break the issues down the following way:

1. Since you are starting your business over, the first thing to do is update your business plan and go back to the bank for a loan. The bank may just be favorable if you include the "new" things you are going to do since the shutdown. Take everything you learn here and make sure your updated business plan captures your new energy and innovations. Identify the steps necessary for refurbishing your business plan. (Suggestion: Move this step to the last if you have decided to start over on your business plan. That way you can benefit from everything you learn in the Checklist and SWOT Analysis. (If you need some help with your business plan, contact my company. I have written over 260 Business Plans and can help you for a small fee. If you'd like to send a copy to me for a quote, send the document as an email attachment to robertsswot@outlook.com.) Or check our website at www.documentservicesinternational.com Determine the business category for this question and place it

under one of the SWOT Analyses, Strengths, Weaknesses, Opportunities and/or Threats.

_____
_____
_____
_____
_____
_____
_____

2. What did the shutdown do to your customer base and what it will likely do to it in the future? Determine the business category for this question and place it under one of the SWOT Analyses, Strengths, Weaknesses, Opportunities and/or Threats.

_____
_____
_____
_____
_____
_____
_____

   a. Let's assume that your business will lose half of its customers due to social distancing. Based upon your average sale in the past, how much will your weekly or monthly revenue be and subtract the projected costs from that number. Now that you know your projected profit, can you survive at that level of profit? Determine the business category for this question and place it under one of the SWOT Analyses, Strengths, Weaknesses, Opportunities and/or Threats. In any event, consider some of the following tactics:

_____
_____

_____
_____
_____
_____
_____
_____
_____

b. Talk to your customers and/or give them a questionnaire on your website so they can tell you what they would like to see you do to ensure they come back to you once you re-open. Offer them a company gift card or other incentive to fill out the questionnaire. Specifically ask what you can do to retain their business. Use this data to define your new business processes. Determine the business category for this question and place it under one of the SWOT Analyses, Strengths, Weaknesses, Opportunities and/or Threats.

_____
_____
_____
_____
_____
_____
_____
_____
_____

c. Look at your past business and ask yourself what you must do to ensure your customers feel 100% safe when returning to your business. Determine the business category for this question and place it under one of the SWOT Analyses, Strengths, Weaknesses, Opportunities and/or Threats.

_____
_____

d. In order to define your new business processes consider the following questions:
   i. How to create distance. Determine the business category for this question and place it under one of the SWOT Analyses, Strengths, Weaknesses, Opportunities and/or Threats.

   ii. What must your employees do to reduce contacts with customers and among themselves – should you get them to sign a "will not sue" contract before they come back to work (check with your lawyer)? Determine the business category for this question and place it under one of the SWOT Analyses, Strengths, Weaknesses, Opportunities and/or Threats.

iii. What new services or products will need to be added
   1. Products not offered before but which can now be offered due to the pandemic – what new needs do customers have that they did not know they now have because of the pandemic? Determine the business category for this question and place it under one of the SWOT Analyses, Strengths, Weaknesses, Opportunities and/or Threats.

   2. Online purchasing. Determine the business category for this question and place it under one of the SWOT Analyses, Strengths, Weaknesses, Opportunities and/or Threats.

3. No touch payment (online credit cards). Determine the business category for this question and place it under one of the SWOT Analyses, Strengths, Weaknesses, Opportunities and/or Threats.

4. Delivery (No touch). Determine the business category for this question and place it under one of the SWOT Analyses, Strengths, Weaknesses, Opportunities and/or Threats.

5. Automatic regular purchases on a schedule. Determine the business category for this question and place it under one of the SWOT Analyses, Strengths, Weaknesses, Opportunities and/or Threats.

6. Seniors – how can you serve them better and provide safety (Remember, not all seniors are technically proficient, so you may have to include some activities to teach them about automatic ordering and include their caretakers in establishing this for them. Determine the business category for this question and place it under one of the SWOT Analyses, Strengths, Weaknesses, Opportunities and/or Threats.

7. What can you invent? (Cubicle enclosed customer areas?) Brainstorm with your employees and ask for their ideas. Determine the business category for this question and place it under one of the SWOT Analyses, Strengths, Weaknesses, Opportunities and/or Threats.

8. Write a letter to your customers telling them what you are doing to ensure they come back. Determine the business category for this question and place it under one of the SWOT Analyses, Strengths, Weaknesses, Opportunities and/or Threats.

9. Improve communication with regular customers and give them discounts and gifts for repeat business – keep the lines of communication open. Determine the business category for this question and place it under one of the SWOT Analyses, Strengths, Weaknesses, Opportunities and/or Threats.

iv. How many customers can you expect based upon the need for distancing? Determine the business category for this question and place it under one of the SWOT Analyses, Strengths, Weaknesses, Opportunities and/or Threats.

1. Don't forget to plan for the time when social distancing is not necessary (once a vaccine is found) – can you hold off doing business at a slower level until then – or must you do something, improve services, add services, invent something new to create a new flow of customers. Determine the business category for this question and place it under one of the SWOT Analyses, Strengths, Weaknesses, Opportunities and/or Threats.

_____
_____
_____
_____
_____
_____
_____

2. Are you targeting the right customers – perhaps there is a new market made possible by the pandemic that you can exploit – begin to probe for this new customer base – necessity is the mother of invention. Determine the business category for this question and place it under one of the SWOT Analyses, Strengths, Weaknesses, Opportunities and/or Threats.

_____
_____
_____
_____
_____
_____

_____
_____
_____

3. Are you going to have the same level of customer "churn" as you did in the past? What is the percent of your budget spent on marketing? Would increasing this gain you new business? Is there a market you ignored before because you were already filling up the joint? Now may be the time to address that market. Determine the business category for this question and place it under one of the SWOT Analyses, Strengths, Weaknesses, Opportunities and/or Threats.

_____
_____
_____
_____
_____
_____
_____

4. What will be the "churn" rate for new customers in the future and how can you manage this rate to ensure profitability? Determine the business category for this question and place it under one of the SWOT Analyses, Strengths, Weaknesses, Opportunities and/or Threats.

_____
_____
_____
_____
_____
_____
_____

5. What must you do in order to correct the loss of business and restore profitability? Determine the business category for this question and place it under

one of the SWOT Analyses, Strengths, Weaknesses, Opportunities and/or Threats.

_____
_____
_____
_____
_____
_____
_____
_____

6. Look at your returning employees. Assess each of their weaknesses and strengths. Who is going to carry you forward toward profitability and who is not? What can you do to improve the effectiveness of each one of them so they are more valuable to the company? Interview each of them and ask them whether they still want to work there. Ask them if they have any suggestions for improving the company? Is there any educational opportunity for either of them so they can be more valuable? Take a good hard look. If you have an employee who cannot contribute or who is a net loss to the business, address this issue with them to identify their level of interest in their job. Determine the business category for this question and place it under one of the SWOT Analyses, Strengths, Weaknesses, Opportunities and/or Threats.

_____
_____
_____
_____
_____
_____
_____
_____

7. Now is the time to reassess your accounts payables and identify areas where savings can be gained. Talk to your creditors and ask them what they can do to help in terms of their receivable policies. Check out your lines

of credit. Ask these people if they can extend those lines or provide more favorable payment terms. Determine the business category for this question and place it under one of the SWOT Analyses, Strengths, Weaknesses, Opportunities and/or Threats.

_____
_____
_____
_____
_____
_____
_____

8. Check your insurance policies. What do they cover? Is there any insurance protection that you can make a claim on due to the pandemic and the economic emergency. Is there a new insurance service that might benefit you in the future? Many insurance companies might be lowering their rates, check out the competition for better terms or lower premiums. Especially check the strength of your lawsuit protections. Are you protected if a customer gets sick and blames it on you? Make sure you have a conference with your insurance company representatives to review all policies in order to protect you against a barrage of lawsuits. Determine the business category for this question and place it under one of the SWOT Analyses, Strengths, Weaknesses, Opportunities and/or Threats.

_____
_____
_____
_____
_____
_____
_____

9. Review your business access points. Things may have changed in terms of the ease of access to your doors,

sidewalks, etc. Keep in mind, the government may be writing a whole new set of regulations for your business that you'll need to accommodate before they let you re-open. These are new costs that could add significantly to the cost of doing business but some of them may actually open an new opportunity for you – so review these matters carefully. Especially, check your bathroom areas and make sure they are squeaky clean and well ventilated. This area could cause you lots of trouble with the local government and customers. Determine the business category for this question and place it under one of the SWOT Analyses, Strengths, Weaknesses, Opportunities and/or Threats.

_____
_____
_____
_____
_____
_____
_____

10. Check your tax status. Does your form of business organization influence your profitability? What new tax regulations or other changes need to be addressed? There are likely even some opportunities afforded by the federal and state taxing authorities that could save you money on your taxes. Make sure you are aware of these changes and identify any easing of tax regulations that might help you. Determine the business category for this question and place it under one of the SWOT Analyses, Strengths, Weaknesses, Opportunities and/or Threats.

_____
_____
_____
_____
_____
_____
_____

11. Check your payment systems. Can they be upgraded to zero-touch? If so, you can create a delivery service for phone and internet orders that will increase business outside of your regular place of business. This would also help people in quarantine and provide additional business among seniors. Determine the business category for this question and place it under one of the SWOT Analyses, Strengths, Weaknesses, Opportunities and/or Threats.

_____
_____
_____
_____
_____
_____
_____
_____

12. Employee training matters that have plagued you over the years should be fixed with new hires with special skills or by taking your returning employees through a training program designed to improve their skills. Determine the business category for this question and place it under one of the SWOT Analyses, Strengths, Weaknesses, Opportunities and/or Threats.

_____
_____
_____
_____
_____
_____
_____
_____

13. Now is the time to put your business processes down on paper so you can create an employee training manual. Learn how to create business processes that work for your business. Take a look at the section in this book on

how to create your business process graphs for every aspect of your business. Determine the business category for this question and place it under one of the SWOT Analyses, Strengths, Weaknesses, Opportunities and/or Threats.

_____
_____
_____
_____
_____
_____
_____

Needless to say, before you conduct your preliminary SWOT Analysis, you must be familiar with every detail of your business and potential weaknesses in your organization, including budget, personnel, volunteers/interns, time, schedule, target audiences, and population sizes of the communities where you do business. If you are not able to do this yourself, then enlist the time and expertise of the individual in your company that you have delegated to perform these activities. This could be a product manager, accountant or marketing manager.

Now that you've gone through your checklist, and taken all your notes, the first thing to do is set up a meeting with your general staff. You want to ask each of them about their biggest problem area to get a good idea of the direction you want to take your first SWOT Analysis. Ask what one problem they would want fixed that would most impact their ability to serve the customer or improve production or lower prices. Take careful notes about who makes which suggestion and get input from the group about which specific problem would be most effective to solve. Gather your notes and then meet with each individual separately and ask him if he were in charge of a specific project, how would he go about running a project team to work on the problem.

SWOT Analysis

Now it is time for your SWOT Analysis. By now you've added all new activities that you identified from your checklist. I suggest you also read some articles from the Internet on suggestions and tips that other experts have identified and decide on activities not covered in your checklist.

Then it will be time to meet with your team for their suggestions and to assign responsibilities for additional action. With the team's help, identify your SMART goals for each activity and your reporting mechanisms (email, text, personal meetings, etc.)

THE STRENGTHS, WEAKNESSES, OPPORTUNITIES AND THREATS ANALYSIS

Strengths

What distinct competencies does your organization bring to your field? Is there anything unique about you that gives you an advantage you can exploit that would continue to give you an edge, or, as Penske would say, to give you the unfair advantage? What additional competencies are possessed by your key employees that might give you an advantage? Or would it be helpful to hire someone with specific competencies that would benefit your company? Consider education, special skills, advanced knowledge? What other resources within the community can you identify that will strengthen your market position? What could you import into your community or business that would make you stronger? Do you have significant support in the community, Better Business Bureau, Rotary Club, Chamber of Commerce, Outreach Programs, Churches, Charities? Can you create a training program for skills that would benefit you? How about a scholarship program to encourage those skills? Can you encourage your local college to add a specific subject to its elective subject curriculum?

Consider all available skills and knowledge that you and your employees have developed in previous positions or the experience of organizing and managing a company. The combination of skills, education, along with a knowledge and interest in the field, certainly provides you with strengths that can help you succeed.

Identify the practical skills and abilities that you or others in your organization may possess. (See Figure 1) Keep in mind, this is not rocket science. Just get a general idea of these skills but also be as specific as you can be. You don't have to take two months to do this. You just want to identify the strengths of your organization as quickly as possible and get it down on paper. It should only take a few minutes. You can add other things that you come up with at a later time.

Outside Strengths

Outside strengths refer to companies with which you do business that provide products or services that you use or sell. You should evaluate these to determine if there is anything that they can do to help you re-start the business more effectively. Even if they have to change a product or service for you, is it something that will give you an edge against your competition?

Keep in mind, these outside companies have been affected by the shutdown and it they want to get back to "normal", they may be very eager to entertain any ideas you have for changes they can make to give you the edge. Talk to them and ask them what have they done in terms of their strategic planning to help you. Ask them what you can do to help them? Is a strategy meeting a good idea. What can you do through remote communication, Skype, or other meeting software to conduct this meeting without having to travel to them.

Also, don't ignore your local universities. Not only can they possibly provide you with new customers, they may have some ideas on how companies can re-engineer themselves to thrive in the post-pandemic period.

Especially consider other companies that are competing with your suppliers or service providers. Learn about what they do and how their products and services compare to what your existing suppliers are providing. Keep abreast of developments. Ask local television and radio programs if they are working on any programming ideas from which you could benefit and or participate. Ask yourself, what can they do to help you?

Back to suppliers, can they "private label" a specific product for you that gives you an edge over the competition? Can they engage in research and development work to find a better material or product feature they can put into your products to make them better? Can they help you improve your efficiency by training you and your employees to be more productive? What are they automating and how are their research and development efforts paying off for them? How can you avail yourself of their knowledge, and, even more importantly, can you independently upgrade their product if you can find an innovation they haven't thought about?

Strengths Analysis Checklist – Figure 1

Assess each skill by writing the term "Strong", "Average" or "Weak" in the Assessment column.

Skill	Assessment
Financial Planning	
Budgeting, Accounting, Management	
Human Resource Management	
Recruiting, Training, Supervising, Motivating Staff and Volunteers	
Safety, Security, Risk Management	
Admissions, Venue Grounds, Spectators, Players, Personnel	
Hospitality	

Invitation Design and Production, Amenities, Coordination of Logistics, Hosting Activities	
Food and Beverage	
Negotiations, Quality, Quantity, Contract and Price	
Sales and Marketing	
Prospecting, Selling, Closing, Servicing	
Writing	
Correspondence, Promotional Copy, Internal Memoranda, Newsletters, Trade Publication Articles, Media Releases, Follow-ups	
Leadership Ability	
List Additional from your Re-start Checklist Below:	

Analysis of Strengths

The first thing to do is organize your strengths in the following order: Strong Assessments, Average Assessments and Weak Assessments. Start with the "weak" assessments and ask your group what ideas they have for improving each of these. Take a "Problem Solving Worksheet" and assign three or more individuals to work on these and report back at next week's meeting. Assign "average" assessment ratings to another group of employees and ask them to report back next week and do likewise with Strong Assessments.

The Problem-Solving Worksheet will give your employees a tool for developing an inductive approach to the problem which will lead to a definitive solution that will be worth discussing. Make sure they are able to develop the necessary audio-visual materials, presentations, charts, business process charts, etc. they would like to present at the next meeting.

Needless to say, your knowledge and leadership will be vital to developing workable solutions that will have a positive influence on the company. Make sure your door is open at all times for any of these team members to walk in and ask questions or hold a discussion with you. Make sure you guide this process and use it as a developmental tool for each individual. Challenge them, never settle for average and push them to go beyond the average and to excel – to find real solutions and develop the arguments necessary to defend their ideas.

At the next SWOT Meeting, give every group an equal amount of time to make their presentation. Don't assign a leader, let the leader emerge and if he takes the baton, let him know it is his baton to carry. Ask the following questions.

On weak assessments:
- Which is the one weakness whose solution will improve the company the most?
- What is the cause of that weakness?
- What can be done to solve it, to turn the weakness into a strength?
- What is the Business Process solution to this weakness? How were things done in the past and how will they be done in the future? Make sure the team uses the Business Process Tool provided in this book so they can make the changes they desire and get it down on paper.
- Why is the proposed solution the best solution?
- What benchmarks will we use to determine success and what kind of reporting mechanism will we use and who will be responsible for the reporting?

Project Worksheet for Strengths

WEEK / DATE	DUTY AND DUE DATE	ASSIGNED TO	DATE FINISHED

SMART Goals for Strength Related Activities (See Appendix if you need additional forms)

Category	Definition	Result and Date of Result
Specific Goal		
Measurable Desired Result		
Achievable (Yes/No)		
Results-Focused (Yes/No)		
Time Bound		

Weaknesses

Analyzing weaknesses, though not an entertaining activity, is vital to your success because these harmful internal weaknesses can negatively impact your success as a company. Additionally, since you were forced to shut down, many things have happened which have affect the economy, other businesses and your markets in particular. If you are going to resume success, you must do everything you can ascertain these new conditions and develop strategies to address them. This part of your SWOT Analysis should be stuffed with all kinds of new weaknesses that you should address.

First, you should convene a meeting with key staff and volunteers to determine any weaknesses that are important enough to address. Go over the lists you developed in your checklist and ask them to suggest solutions. Ask them about internal areas that are inadequate, that may be controlled and/or corrected, or that should be eliminated before they erode your profitability. Tell them this is their opportunity to create a business that will make money for all team members and tie them to success.

Elimination of weaknesses may mean personnel changes, retraining or reassignment, possibly even termination of some people and hiring someone with special skills. Weaknesses and dealing with them are as important to your organization as strengths because they are the negatives that are drawing you down.

One weakness to seriously look at: Is your marketing program good enough to bring in new customers or sales now that you are returning?

Use Figure 2 for identifying weaknesses of your team.

The Weakness Analysis Checklist - Figure 2

Weakness	Assessment
Disagreements among key staff and/or volunteers	
Personality conflicts among staff and/or volunteers	
Lack of trained, experienced personnel and/or volunteers	
Short planning time	
Funding problems	
Facility shortage or inadequacies	
Other weaknesses (list)	

Don't forget to include weaknesses in the supplier chain that have come up during the shutdown. They may need internal fixes or the development of a new supply chain. Also look at every product or service and ask whether the new market for it is still there and/or if you need to re-engineer it and market it differently.

This approach of assessing your company strengths and weaknesses will help you improve your organization and enable you to handle the opportunities and threats from both inside and outside sources. This is critical to the survival of your company and your future success. If you don't know what is wrong, you don't know how to fix it. If you don't know your weaknesses, you don't know how to turn them into strengths. This is what I call focused management and it is much better than just plodding along, don't you think?

On weak assessments:

Which is the one weakness whose solution will improve the company the most?

_____
_____
_____
_____
_____
_____

What is the cause of that weakness?

_____
_____
_____
_____
_____
_____

What can be done to solve it, to turn the weakness into a strength?

_____
_____
_____
_____
_____
_____

What is the Business Process solution to this weakness? How were things done in the past and how will they be done in the future?

_____
_____
_____
_____
_____

Why is the proposed solution the best solution?

_____
_____
_____
_____
_____

What benchmarks will we use to determine success and what kind of reporting mechanism will you use and who will be responsible for the reporting?

_____
_____
_____
_____
_____

Project Worksheet for Weaknesses

WEEK / DATE	DUTY AND DUE DATE	ASSIGNED TO	DATE FINISHED

SMART Goals for Weaknesses

Category	Definition	Result and Date of Result
Specific Goal		
Measurable Desired Result		
Achievable (Yes/No)		
Results-Focused (Yes/No)		
Time Bound		

Opportunities

The opportunities that present themselves post pandemic may help you restore your revenues to previous levels or higher, but what are these opportunities? How can you recognize them, anticipate them and plan for them?

- Local Opportunities – Your local area has a strong base of businesses with which you can develop strong relationships – find out how to meet the necessary people and where to hang out so you can meet the Who's Who in local influence. You can try to meet them via social media or chat services to reduce the need to meet in public.

- These are all good people to know. As I mentioned above, a good place to start is your local golf club (once it opens). One executive I knew years ago told me he got lots of his clients by sitting at the bar of his golf club one or two nights a week. You might be surprised who shows up at places where people gather for fun and relaxation.

- Don't forget social networking sites. I've had lots of my Facebook friends turn into clients because I sometimes posted work my company had done for other clients. You can create your own social media network and meet lots of new people by careful postings on Facebook, Twitter and/or LinkedIn.com. Don't forget local business groups such as Kiwanis, Toastmasters and others where you can meet intelligent and industrious people intent on self-improvement and making good connections. Your local Chamber of Commerce and other similar organizations can be helpful as well. We mentioned some of them in the Checklist.

- Events as opportunities – Every event you participate in or put on, and even those you don't, often present opportunities to meet people who can help you, or people with whom you can network. Remember, many of these people are struggling to restart their businesses too. Are you ready for these opportunities? Do you have a plan to pursue them and take advantage of them?

You will want to qualify all opportunities as "HOT" (action required), "GREEN" (investigate further) and "LUKEWARM" (possible but not immediate need). Finally, determine whether an opportunity requires action on your part to make it happen.

Use Figure 3 to identify the opportunities for your business.

Opportunity	Assessment
Each planned event (list below – include Trade Shows, Seminars, Job Fairs, etc.)	
New Opportunities (list below)	

Opportunities you have identified from your checklist should each support your goals and objectives of restarting your business. If one does not *entirely* support your end-result, determine ways to control it or get rid of it. For example, a tourist-related activity such as a major music festival may be scheduled on the same date as your concert or sporting event. Control this activity to the best of your ability by giving your local fans and sponsors something special that day so they come to your event rather than the festival. Or have flyers passed out at the festival telling people about your event to see how many decide to do both. If they present the flyer at a place of your designation, give them a freebie for coming. Otherwise, this scheduling conflict could become a threat rather than an opportunity.

Additional suggestions:

There may be opportunities of which you are unaware and the world of the Internet can provide you with valuable information about new opportunities. I would suggest that you use the following keywords on your favorite search engine:

Trade Shows

Seminars

Sales Training

Press Releases (in your industry)

Open Projects and Grant Opportunities

Also use keywords that are typical in your industry.

I would even recommend having one of your marketing employees check these and other keywords every day and report his or her findings to the VP of Marketing. You might be surprised about what you can discover that will be very valuable to your revenues.

Project Worksheet for Opportunities

WEEK / DATE	DUTY AND DUE DATE	ASSIGNED TO	DATE FINISHED

SMART Goals for Opportunities

Category	Definition	Result and Date of Result
Specific Goal		
Measurable Desired Result		
Achievable (Yes/No)		
Results-Focused (Yes/No)		
Time Bound		

Threats

Threats of all types may jeopardize the success of your business. By recognizing potential threats, you gain the advantage of planning ahead and blocking these threats from harming your business. Certainly, you want to check out the local political environment. Are judges and politicians prone to restricting your ability to open your business intelligently or are they more free-market oriented. Either situation could have an impact over whether you should give it a try.

Also check the banking relationships you have. Can you get a new line of credit? What about your own line of credit? Do you want to keep it for the "usual cash flow" situation or should you take a risk on using it to re-open? This may be a "no brainer" for you but consider all your options. It pays to have an insurance policy as they say.

To determine the range of threats to your success, bring together all team members for a threat analysis meeting. This includes risk management, volunteers, marketing people, mechanics, engineers, technicians and all other critical people.

Ask each employee to list any potential threats within their area of responsibility and identify any threats that may affect the company as a whole. I've always told my people, if you give me a problem, bring the solution with you. That will help motivate them to make a contribution. See Figure 4.

The Threats Analysis Checklist Figure 4

Threats	Comments and Solutions (Criteria: Serious, Monitor Further, Requires Action
Personnel	
Business Processes	
Rules and Regulations	
Financial Concerns	
Sales	
Management	
Customer Service	
Other Threats (list)	

Project Worksheet for Threats

WEEK / DATE	DUTY AND DUE DATE	ASSIGNED TO	DATE FINISHED

SMART Goals for Threats

Category	Definition	Result and Date of Result
Specific Goal		
Measurable Desired Result		
Achievable (Yes/No)		
Results-Focused (Yes/No)		
Time Bound		

Now that you've finished your SWOT Analysis, enlist your team in a project that will assign an action, a completion date and a "report-back" date for each initiative you will assign to them. Keep records of all this and set schedule items for yourself to follow up on all acts and ascertain how things are going.

Business Process Analysis

The work of creating business processes can be a long and hard one for many managers and owners. Yet, it is vital to the success of any business that it have specific and precise processes available for all employees especially management.

In this chapter, we are going to present some examples of how to "graph" a business process and how to determine the steps necessary to see the process into action. Let's get an overview of the process development process.

1. Start at the end. What specific value does your business require that you need a business process for?
2. Identify the steps that an employee or manager will take in order to accomplish that business value.
3. Occam's Razor. Specify, simplify, minimize these steps. Which steps can be accomplished simultaneously?
4. Technologize, computerize, program, productize. Identify the technologies available in the marketplace and identify those which a) accomplish the process, b) reduce steps and c) provide the least or zero contact between the customer and the employee.

Example: Lead Development Process
We are going to start with a high-level business process so you can get a "big-picture" perspective on business process development. We're going to take each step individually.
1. Start at the end. What specific value does your business require that you need a business process for?
   We need an effective process for identifying business leads and moving those leads toward sales and mutually beneficial business relationships.
2. Identify the steps that an employee or manager will take in order to accomplish that business value.

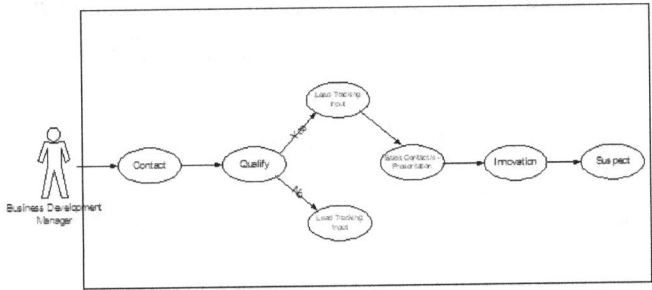

3. Occam's Razor. Specify, simplify, minimize these steps. Which steps can be accomplished simultaneously?
   Let's identify contact management software items that may help in this process and create a team to evaluate and access those products for our purposes.
4. Technologize, computerize, program, productize. Identify the technologies available in the marketplace and identify those which a) accomplish the process, b) reduce steps and c) provide the least or zero contact between the customer and the employee.
   This is the challenge. Can this process be re-imagined so that we eliminate all personal contacts? If not, what are the minimal contacts that are absolutely necessary? How can we re-engineer the process? Can we develop a "short-term" solution until the need for "zero-touch" passes?

As you can see, the last step is the most important step because it utilizes all the information and resources you have imagined for the business process and reduced it to the purpose of re-imagining your business as a "zero-touch" business. If you can successfully impact your business with these adjustments, you may have invented a process that you can take forward into the future, or, at the very least, you'll have something that will tide you over until you are able to do the job in the "normal" way. This gives you plenty of options for the future. Either you've found an efficiency that is less costly or that can be enhanced later when "normal" business processes can resume. The tables below can show you the way.

Ref	Requirement	Consumed	Created	Priority
1.1	Lead generation and sales processing			1
	a. Contact	• Client Profiles • Client Sales Letters • Non-disclosure Agreement	• New Prospect Profile	
	b. Lead Qualification – Yes or No	• Client Profiles • External Databases	• New Prospect Profile	
	c. Input into Lead Tracking System	• Lead Tracking Template	• Lead Tracking Form	

Villegas Decision-Making Worksheet

Every decision you make should be based upon the relevant facts of the situation that gives rise to the need for a decision. These facts can be broken down into positive statements (propositions and conclusions) that can be checked against reality (proven). You arrive at these conclusions and propositions by means of investigation (also called induction).

Effective decision-making can only take place when you use the best available knowledge. The jump from your knowledge to the correct decision is much easier if you apply the principles we discussed in our chapters on logic and logical fallacies.

Decision-making can only be based upon induction and analysis of the facts of reality as they relate to the field upon which you must decide. Essentially, there are three steps:

1. Identify the question about which the decision is to be made, and

2. Identify the facts that relate to that question, and

3. Identify the team members who have the expertise to help in making the decision

4. Draw your conclusion

5. Assign and schedule all actions

6. Schedule followups

Villegas Decision-Making Worksheet

Villegas Decision-Making Worksheet
Date:
Individuals involved in this decision
Question
Relevant Facts
Needed Knowledge
How Will You Apply this Knowledge?

What tests or analyses will I need to make?
Results of test or analysis – list as bullet points
Decision (give reasons)
Who will implement the decision?

How will the decision be implemented?
When will the decision be implemented?
Who will be responsible for maintaining any necessary actions and to whom will they report?
When will the follow-up take place and who will do it?

Villegas Problem Solving Worksheet

In this section, we refer to business problems that haunt the company. They can be such things as inefficient business processes, the use of faulty equipment in production, personnel policies and standards of quality, etc. Such problems cause a business to lose money, perform disappointingly or harm company morale. When a business problem is solved, the company becomes stronger and improves its standing with customers.

As an employee, you add value to the company when you consider yourself part of the solution rather than part of the problem. Problem solving is a skill that all the best managers have. They don't hold back and they never settle for situations that keep the company from fulfilling its mission.

The first thing to do to solve a business problem is to describe the problem and the negative consequences of the problem. Quantify these consequences if possible. Then, use the process of induction to identify a solution that has a "possible" better consequence.

Implementing the solution is also very important. Someone should be charged with the responsibility for taking the actions that will solve the problem and a reporting process should be maintained. As this process moves forward, adjustments should be made as needed to improve the solution and focus it specifically on the problem.

It is always important to realize that it is the boss's or owner's responsibility to sanction your work and make the final decision to change procedures and fix the problem. Make sure you have his or her blessing for anything you do to solve the problem.

Villegas Problem Solving Worksheet

Villegas Problem Solving Worksheet
Date:
Individuals involved in this investigation
Problem
Statistics or Measurement Criteria
What is the Specific Cause of this Problem?

What is the Specific Business Process that is affected by this Problem?

Describe the Steps of this Business Process

What Specific Step is Responsible for this Problem?

What New Step/s Will Solve this Problem?

Describe the New Business Process with the New Steps

Perform some tests of this new procedure and measure the result. Then calculate the effect of the new procedure if all people performing this process were to do so.

Meet with and Report Results to the Director in Charge. Report the Results of the Meeting Here:

Next Step: (Do Another Worksheet or Implement the Procedure Company-Wide)

SWOT Analysis as a Performance Review

You can use a SWOT Analysis to investigate company-wide problems or specific problems that plague a department or small group of employees. You can also use a SWOT Analysis as a Performance Review for an individual. Such a review would have the added benefit of not only evaluating the employee but also giving him or her a plan for improving their performance based upon the employee's chosen areas for improvement and helping to set a follow up for him or her within a few months. Below are the four steps that I recommend for a Performance Review. Of course, you can also create one specific to the tasks that any individual must address in his or her own performance.

Strengths

Weaknesses

Opportunities

Threats

Once you have identified each element then the next step is to identify what the employee must do in order to deal with each element.

Element	Characteristics	Planned Action and Date	Date Completed
Strengths			
Weaknesses			
Opportunities			
Threats			

Performance Review

The Personal SWOT Analysis

The SWOT Analysis can also provide the foundation for your personal and career development. A well-thought-out SWOT Analysis can keep you on track in your career and keep you ahead of the game when it comes to the expectations of your boss. I'd also recommend your obtaining a copy of my book: "How to be a Great Employee and a Better Manager".

Personal SWOT Analysis			
Element	Characteristics	Planned Action and Date	Date Completed
Strengths			
Weaknesses			
Opportunities			
Threats			

Appendix: Checklists and Forms

Restart Checklist Blank Form

This new Restart SWOT Analysis involves two specific analyses that you must undertake right now. The first involves identifying the specific challenges that the shutdown created for your business. To help with this we have provided above a checklist of issues you should address before you re-open.

Once you finish this initial checklist, look over it carefully and make any change and adjustments you'd like before you present it to your management team or staff. This will serve as the basis for your SWOT Analysis.

First, you must identify as much as possible what the shutdown did to your business, not only to your customer base, but also your business and the market in which you operate, and what it will likely do in the future.

_____
_____
_____
_____
_____

Are you going to have the same level of customer "churn" as you did in the past? What will be the "churn" rate for new customers be in the future and how can you manage this rate to ensure profitability?

_____
_____
_____
_____
_____

Next, what must you do in order to correct the loss of business and restore profitability?

_____
_____
_____
_____
_____
_____
_____

So, let's break the issues down the following way:

14. Since you are starting your business over, the first thing to do is update your business plan and go back to the bank for a loan. The bank may just be favorable if you include the "new" things you are going to do since the shutdown. Take everything you learn here and make sure your updated business plan captures your new energy and innovations. Identify the steps necessary for refurbishing your business plan. (Suggestion: Move this step to the last if you have decided to start over on your business plan.

_____
_____
_____
_____
_____
_____

15. What did the shutdown do to your customer base and what it will likely do to it in the future?

_____
_____
_____
_____
_____

e. Let's assume that your business will lose half of its customers due to social distancing. Based upon your average sale in the past, how much will your weekly or monthly revenue be and subtract the projected costs from that number. Now that you know your projected profit, can you survive at that level of profit? In any event, consider some of the following tactics:

f. Talk to your customers and/or give them a questionnaire on your website so they can tell you what they would like to see you do to ensure they come back to you once you re-open. Offer them a company gift card or other incentive to fill out the questionnaire. Specifically ask what you can do to retain their business. Use this data to define your new business processes.

g. Look at your past business and ask yourself what you must do to ensure your customers feel 100% safe when returning to your business.

h. In order to define your new business processes consider the following questions:
   i. How to create distance

   ii. What must your employees do to reduce contacts with customers and among themselves – should you get them to sign a "will not sue" contract before they come back to work (check with your lawyer)?

iii. What new services or products will need to be added
    1. Products not offered before but which can now be offered due to the pandemic – what new needs do customers have that they did not know they now have because of the pandemic?

    2. Online purchasing

    3. No touch payment (online credit cards)

4. Delivery (No touch)

5. Automatic regular purchases on a schedule

6. Seniors – how can you serve them better and provide safety (Remember, not all seniors are technically proficient, so you may have to include some activities to teach them about automatic ordering and include their caretakers in establishing this for them.

_____
_____
_____
_____
_____

7. What can you invent? (Cubicle enclosed customer areas?) Brainstorm with your employees and ask for their ideas

_____
_____
_____
_____
_____
_____

8. Write a letter to your customers telling them what you are doing to ensure they come back

_____
_____
_____
_____
_____
_____

9. Improve communication with regular customers and give them discounts and gifts for repeat business – keep the lines of communication open

iv. How many customers can you expect based upon the need for distancing?

1. Don't forget to plan for the time when social distancing is not necessary (once a vaccine is found) – can you hold off doing business at a slower level until then – or must you do something, improve services, add services, invent something new to create a new flow of customers

2. Are you targeting the right customers – perhaps there is a new market made possible by the pandemic that you can exploit – begin to probe for this new customer base – necessity is the mother of invention

_____
_____
_____
_____
_____
_____

16. Are you going to have the same level of customer "churn" as you did in the past? What is the percent of your budget spent on marketing? Would increasing this gain you new business? Is there a market you ignored before because you were already filling up the joint? Now may be the time to address that market.

_____
_____
_____
_____
_____
_____

17. What will be the "churn" rate for new customers in the future and how can you manage this rate to ensure profitability?

_____
_____
_____
_____
_____
_____

18. What must you do in order to correct the loss of business and restore profitability?

_____
_____
_____
_____
_____
_____

19. Look at your returning employees. Assess each of their weaknesses and strengths. Who is going to carry you forward toward profitability and who is not? What can you do to improve the effectiveness of each one of them so they are more valuable to the company? Interview each of them and ask them whether they still want to work there. Ask them if they have any suggestions for improving the company? Is there any educational opportunity for either of them so they can be more valuable? Take a good hard look. If you have an employee who cannot contribute or who is a net loss to the business, address this issue with them to identify their level of interest in their job.

_____
_____
_____
_____
_____
_____

20. Now is the time to reassess your accounts payables and identify areas where savings can be gained. Talk to your creditors and ask them what they can do to help in terms of their receivable policies. Check out your lines of credit. Ask these people if they can extend those lines or provide more favorable payment terms.

_____
_____
_____

21. Check your insurance policies. What do they cover? Is there any insurance protection that you can make a claim on due to the pandemic and the economic emergency. Is there a new insurance service that might benefit you in the future? Many insurance companies might be lowering their rates, check out the competition for better terms or lower premiums. Especially check the strength of your lawsuit protections. Are you protected if a customer gets sick and blames it on you? Make sure you have a conference with your insurance company representatives to review all policies in order to protect you against a barrage of lawsuits.

22. Review your business access points. Things may have changed in terms of the ease of access to your doors, sidewalks, etc. Keep in mind, the government may be writing a whole new set of regulations for your business that you'll need to accommodate before they let you re-open. These are new costs that could add significantly to the cost of doing business but some of them may actually open an new opportunity for you – so review these matters carefully. Especially, check your bathroom areas and make sure they are squeaky clean and well ventilated. This area could cause you lots of trouble with the local government and customers.

23. Check your tax status. Does your form of business organization influence your profitability? What new tax regulations or other changes need to be addressed? There are likely even some opportunities afforded by the federal and state taxing authorities that could save you money on your taxes. Make sure you are aware of these changes and identify any easing of tax regulations that might help you.

24. Check your payment systems. Can they be upgraded to zero-touch? If so, you can create a delivery service for phone and internet orders that will increase business outside of your regular place of business. This would also help people in quarantine and provide additional business among seniors.

25. Employee training matters that have plagued you over the years should be fixed with new hires with special skills or by taking your returning employees through a training program designed to improve their skills.

26. Now is the time to put your business processes down on paper so you can create an employee training manual. Learn how to create business processes that work for your business. Take a look at the section in this book on how to create your business process graphs for every aspect of your business.

Needless to say, before you conduct your preliminary SWOT Analysis, you must be familiar with every detail of your business and potential weaknesses in your organization, including budget, personnel, volunteers/interns, time, schedule, target audiences, and population sizes of the communities where you do business. If you are not able to do this yourself, then enlist the time and expertise of the individual in your company that you have delegated to perform these activities. This could be a product manager, accountant or marketing manager.

Now that you've gone through your checklist, and taken all your notes, the first thing to do is set up a meeting with your general staff. You want to ask each of them about their biggest problem area to get a good idea of the direction you want to take your first SWOT Analysis. Ask what one problem they would want fixed that would most impact their ability to serve the customer or improve production or lower prices. Take careful notes about who makes which suggestion and get input from the group about which specific problem would be most effective to solve. Gather your notes and then meet with each individual separately and ask him if he were in charge of a specific project, how would he go about running a project team to work on the problem.

SMART Goals Worksheet

SMART Goals Worksheet		
Category	**Definition**	**Result and Date of Result**
Specific Goal		
Measurable Desired Result		
Achievable (Yes/No)		
Results-Focused (Yes/No)		
Time Bound		

SMART Goals Worksheet		
Category	Definition	Result and Date of Result
Specific Goal		
Measurable Desired Result		
Achievable (Yes/No)		
Results-Focused (Yes/No)		
Time Bound		

SMART Goals Worksheet		
Category	Definition	Result and Date of Result
Specific Goal		

Measurable Desired Result		
Achievable (Yes/No)		
Results-Focused (Yes/No)		
Time Bound		

SMART Goals Worksheet		
Category	Definition	Result and Date of Result
Specific Goal		
Measurable Desired Result		
Achievable (Yes/No)		

Results-Focused (Yes/No)		
Time Bound		

Project Worksheet

Project Worksheet

WEEK / DATE	DUTY AND DUE DATE	ASSIGNED TO	DATE FINISHED

Villegas Decision-Making Worksheet

Villegas Decision-Making Worksheet
Date:
Individuals involved in this decision
Question
Relevant Facts
Needed Knowledge
How Will You Apply this Knowledge?

What tests or analyses will I need to make?
Results of test or analysis – list as bullet points
Decision (give reasons)
Who will implement the decision?
How will the decision be implemented?

When will the decision be implemented?
Who will be responsible for maintaining any necessary actions and to whom will they report?
When will the follow-up take place and who will do it?

Villegas Problem Solving Worksheet

Villegas Problem Solving Worksheet
Date:
Individuals involved in this investigation
Problem
Statistics or Measurement Criteria
What is the Specific Cause of this Problem?

What is the Specific Business Process that is affected by this Problem?
Describe the Steps of this Business Process
What Specific Step is Responsible for this Problem?
What New Step/s Will Solve this Problem?

Describe the New Business Process with the New Steps

Perform some tests of this new procedure and measure the result. Then calculate the effect of the new procedure if all people performing this process were to do so.

Meet with and Report Results to the Director in Charge. Report the Results of the Meeting Here:

Next Step: (Do Another Worksheet or Implement the Procedure Company-Wide)

Performance Review

	Performance Review		
Element	Characteristics	Planned Action and Date	Date Completed
Strengths			
Weaknesses			
Opportunities			
Threats			

Personal SWOT Analysis

\	Personal SWOT Analysis		
Element	Characteristics	Planned Action and Date	Date Completed
Strengths			
Weaknesses			
Opportunities			

Threats			

Remote Workers for your Business

Development and Business Environments

Development and business environments range across the full spectrum of work environments gaining the benefit of accommodating the needs of the best professionals in the technology fields. The suggestions below are part of my book Website Development Methodologies and it spells out a "traditional" work environment comprised of central server, on site employees and remote employees all connected to the main knowledge and document management servers. This environment (or something like it) is something you may want to consider for your business especially if you have employees who could do their jobs remotely from home or through their laptops anywhere in the world.

Development and Business Center

The development center environment is a full-fledged network center whose only goal is the management of corporate work environments and client systems. (See next page) It is designed to enable E-commerce, developer, CRM helpdesks and CRM call center environments, as well as other professionals to have access to the latest in development tools and hardware while working in a corporate and team environment. The Development and Business Center is the hub of the business. It houses all the necessary software, storage of documents and database storage equipment.

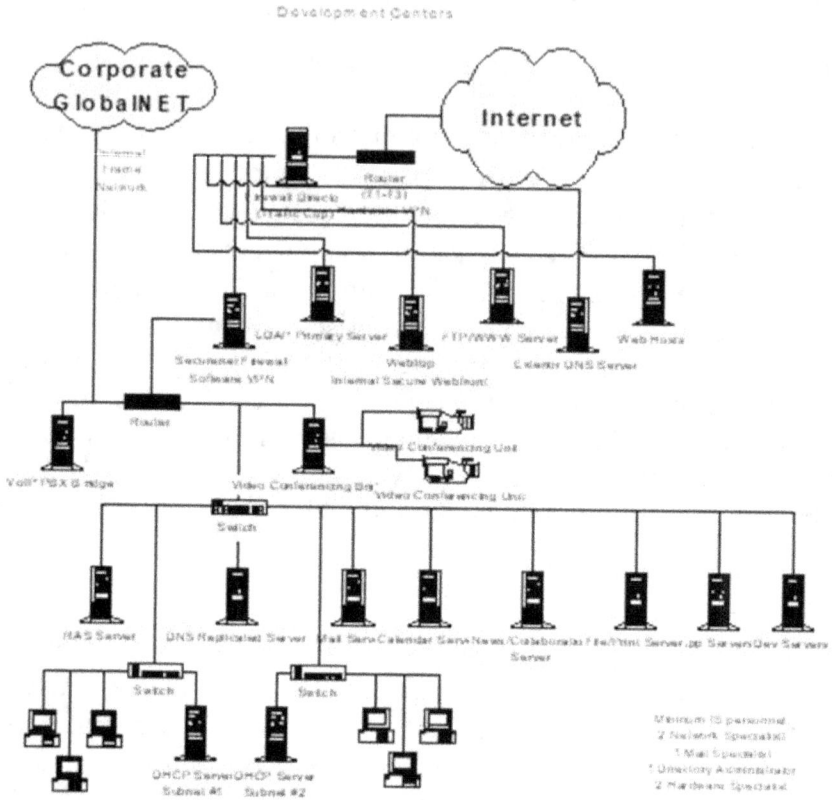

Figure 1. The Development and Business Center Environment

The Remote Environment

The remote environment enables the use of regional or local talent in some of the best technology centers around the world. This environment enables technology workers to gravitate toward those centers where the technology jobs reside and it enables the design firm to effectively contract with them for their services.

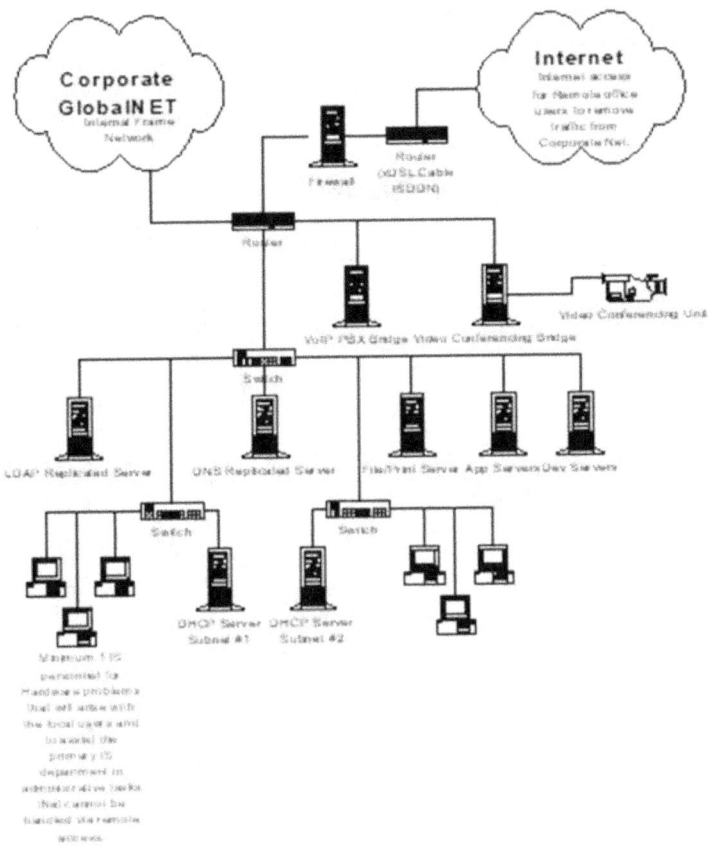

Figure 2. The Remote Environment

The Virtual Employee

The virtual office enables highly talented employees to work from home or a local office. This environment is useful for needed employees who would prefer not to relocate or those who may be travel-challenged.

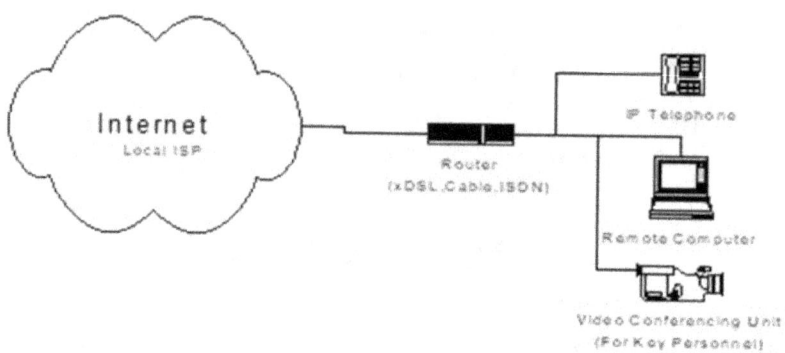

Figure 3. The Virtual Employee

Conclusion

Companies that don't change don't survive. Change can come after recognizing a competitor's success or by careful planning through tools such as the SWOT Analysis, SMART goals and well-documented project management. It pays to become proficient at changing to meet your customers' needs especially in an environment when government can put an end to the economy at a moment's notice.

If you have any questions about this booklet, don't hesitate to send an email to robertsswot@outlook.com. If we add your ideas to this book, we will give you credit and link to your website. If you have a great success story, perhaps we can profile your experience in future versions of this publication or on our website.

Much success to you.

About Robert Villegas

Robert Villegas is an American writer born in Weslaco, TX. He has also served in the US Military as a communications specialist and served his tour of duty during the Vietnam era in Korea near the DMZ. He was raised in Indiana and presently lives in Arizona.

Mr. Villegas spent over twenty-seven years as a UPS executive in Indiana and worked in locations all over Europe such as Germany, England and Spain. After leaving UPS, Mr. Villegas started his own sport marketing company specializing in writing sponsorship proposals for race car drivers and other athletes. He also worked as a technical writer in the burgeoning telecommunications industry in South Florida where he created many successful sales presentations and marketing documents. He also built his company's first website and worked for companies throughout the country including New York City, Boston, San Francisco, Sacramento, Chicago, Miami, Minneapolis, Vancouver BC and other locations.

In 2015, he began to pursue his life-long goal of becoming a published author and has written about 74 books to date in areas such as novels, theater, religion, poetry, philosophy and business. During this period, he also wrote over 260 Business Plans mostly for companies in Canada. He also wrote grant proposals and developed grant proposal narratives for several organizations, earning millions of dollars for fire departments and charitable organizations.

He was educated in Indiana and earned a Degree through the University of the State of NY (Albany) via an external degree program. He is divorced with three grown children and three grandchildren. Famous relatives include Mexican anti-hero Dimas DeLeon and guitarist and music producer Johnny Garcia of Weslaco, TX (lead guitarist for Garth Brooks and Trisha Yearwood).

His favorite author is Ayn Rand and he is an avid movie-buff presently looking for a production company to make movies from his stories and historical works.

Business Books by Robert Villegas

These four books by Robert Villegas comprise some of the business books that he has written. As an executive working for several companies, he was able to develop these methods that will help anyone seeking to excel in the business world. These books are:

How to Be a Great Employee – and a Greater Manager

You cannot be a great manager without first being a great employee. And this is something that requires learning, experience and attitude. The attitude comes from you but the learning and experience you should acquire through diligent study and practice. http://amzn.to/2BqdG2i $3.99 Kindle $8.95 softcover

SWOT Analysis Supercharged

A SWOT Analysis is an objective look at the internal and external elements of your organization that impact your success or lack thereof. If done diligently, you will always have a handle on what you need to do to improve season after season.
http://amzn.to/2BCAWYx $3.99 Kindle $6.95 softcover

The Five-Module Call Center Training System

The Five-Module Call Center Training System is designed to assist the Call Center Team Leader in helping his employees quickly upgrade their skills to an acceptable level. http://amzn.to/2B3Svj1 $3.99 Kindle $5.95 softcover

Website Development Methodology

Effective strategic marketing requires the ability to differentiate the website development organization and its deliverables from those of the competition. http://amzn.to/2DnYMqh $2.99 Kindle $12.95 softcover.

www.robertvillegas.com

www.ingramcontent.com/pod-product-compliance
Lightning Source LLC
Chambersburg PA
CBHW070250220526
45465CB00004B/1568